500 FACTS
OCEANS

500 FACTS
OCEANS

First published in 2010 by Miles Kelly Publishing Ltd
Harding's Barn, Bardfield End Green, Thaxted, Essex, CM6 3PX, UK

2 4 6 8 10 9 7 5 3 1

Editorial Director Belinda Gallagher
Art Director Jo Brewer
Cover Designer Simon Lee
Designers Joe Jones, Simon Lee,
Andrea Slane, Elaine Wilkinson
Editors Carly Blake, Rosie McGuire,
Sarah Parkin, Claire Philip
Indexer Indexing Specialists (UK) Ltd
Production Manager Elizabeth Collins
Reprographics Anthony Cambray, Stephan Davis,
Jennifer Hunt, Liberty Newton, Ian Paulyn
Assets Manager Bethan Ellish
Contributors Camilla de la Bedoyere, Fiona Macdonald,
David Parham, Steve Parker

ISBN 978-1-84810-309-2

Printed in China

British Library Cataloguing-in-Publication Data
A catalogue record for this book is available from the British Library

Made with paper from a sustainable forest

www.mileskelly.net
info@mileskelly.net

www.factsforprojects.com

Self-publish your
children's book

buddingpress.co.uk

Contents

DEEP OCEAN 92–133

WHALES AND DOLPHINS 134–175

The edge of the land

1 **Seashores can be found all over the world, from icy coastlines near the Poles to sandy beaches in hot, tropical areas.** As well as making unique habitats (natural homes) for many plants and animals, seashores are also very important to people. Today, large areas of Earth's 700,000-plus kilometres of seashores are in danger and in need of our protection.

▼ Tall columns of rock (stacks), tidal pools, seaweeds and starfish are typical of rocky shores. This peaceful summer scene is at Second Beach near La Push, Washington State, USA.

Land meets sea

2 Seashores are places where the salty water of seas and oceans meets land made of rocks, mud, sand or other material. A seashore is the edge of the land and the edge of the sea.

Wave-shaped icebergs, Iceland

ARCTIC OCEAN

NORTH AMERICA

Tourist centre, Mexico

PACIFIC OCEAN

ATLANTIC OCEAN

3 There are names for different kinds of seashores. If the rocks are tall and upright, they are known as cliffs. If the sand is smooth and slopes gently, it is a beach. Seashores are known as oceanic coasts, or marine or sea coastlines.

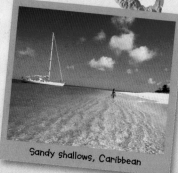
Sandy shallows, Caribbean

SOUTH AMERICA

4 Water moves easily with waves, tides and currents, so seashores are never still. They are complicated habitats for nature, as only certain kinds of animals and plants can live there. Wildlife must be able to survive in the changing conditions that are typical of most seashores.

Breaking glaciers, Antarctica

SOUTHERN OCEAN

Seafront houses, Denmark

ASIA

EUROPE

PACIFIC OCEAN

AFRICA

Tropical palm beach, Seychelles

Great Barrier Reef, Australia

INDIAN OCEAN

OCEANIA

5 There are more than 700,000 kilometres of seashore. Canada is the country with the longest total seashore, at more than 202,000 kilometres. Indonesia is next, with 55,000 kilometres of seashore.

6 Some seashores are not part of the world's main network of seas and oceans. They are the seashores around the edges of large bodies of salty water that are isolated inland, such as the Caspian Sea and the Dead Sea.

ANTARCTICA

Endless battles

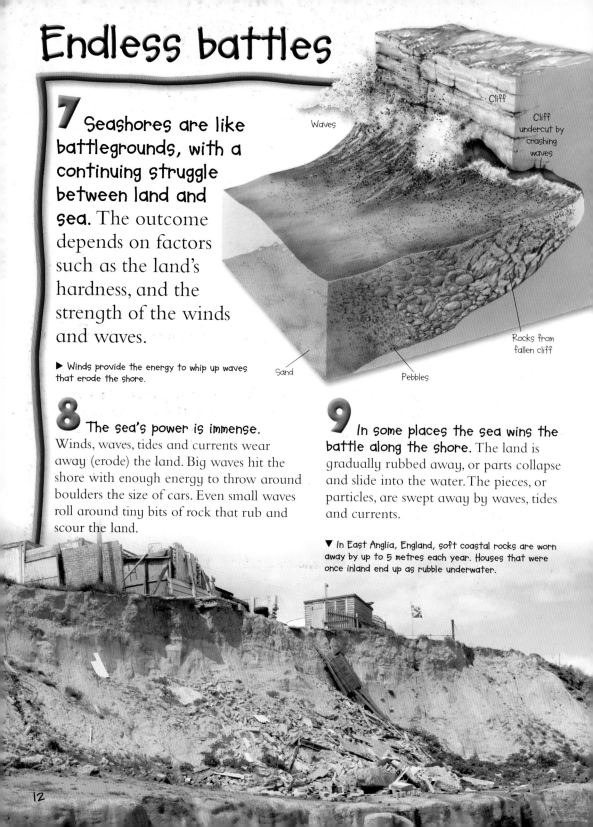

7 Seashores are like battlegrounds, with a continuing struggle between land and sea. The outcome depends on factors such as the land's hardness, and the strength of the winds and waves.

▶ Winds provide the energy to whip up waves that erode the shore.

Waves

Cliff

Cliff undercut by crashing waves

Rocks from fallen cliff

Sand

Pebbles

8 The sea's power is immense. Winds, waves, tides and currents wear away (erode) the land. Big waves hit the shore with enough energy to throw around boulders the size of cars. Even small waves roll around tiny bits of rock that rub and scour the land.

9 In some places the sea wins the battle along the shore. The land is gradually rubbed away, or parts collapse and slide into the water. The pieces, or particles, are swept away by waves, tides and currents.

▼ In East Anglia, England, soft coastal rocks are worn away by up to 5 metres each year. Houses that were once inland end up as rubble underwater.

▲ These granite rocks in Nova Scotia, Canada, have hardly changed for hundreds of years.

▲ Chalk cliffs in southern England are eaten away by waves, leaving piles of broken pieces at their bases.

10 How the seashore's land resists the eroding power of the sea depends on the types of rocks. Hard rocks, such as granite, are tough and can resist erosion for centuries. Softer rocks, such as chalk and mudstone, erode several metres each year.

11 In other places, the land wins the battle. New land can be formed from piles of particles, such as sand or silt, moved by the water from coasts elsewhere or from the deep sea. Particles sink and settle as layers, called sediments, that build up.

12 Movements in the Earth can change seashores. Land can bend and buckle over centuries, so coasts slowly rise. Earthquakes can lift land by several metres in a few seconds. A volcano near the coast can spill its red–hot lava into the sea, where it cools as hard, new rock.

▶ Lava meets the sea in Hawaii. Sea water makes volcanic lava cool suddenly in a cloud of steam.

CLIFF COLLAPSE!

You will need:
large, deep tray or bowl
wet play sand   water

Make a steep cliff in the tray or bowl by piling up wetted sand on one side. Then gently pour in the water. Swish the water with your hand to make waves. Watch how they eat into the cliff and make it fall down.

13

Tides, currents and winds

13 Almost all seashores have tides, which affect the way the land is worn away. Tides alter the amount of time that a particular patch of the shore is underwater or exposed to the air, so they also affect coastal habitats and wildlife.

14 Tides are caused by the pulling power or gravity of the Moon and Sun, and the daily spinning of the Earth. A high tide occurs about 12.5 hours after the previous high tide, with low tides midway between.

Moon

Spinning Earth

Tidal bulge

◀ The Moon's gravity pulls the sea into 'bulges' on the near and opposite sides, where it is high tide. Inbetween is low tide. As the Earth spins daily, the 'bulge' travels around the planet.

I DON'T BELIEVE IT!

The tidal range is the difference in height between high and low tide. In the Bay of Fundy in Canada it is 17 metres, and in parts of the Mediterranean Sea it is less than 0.3 metres.

15 Spring tides are extra-high — the water level rises more than normal. They happen when the Moon and Sun are in line with the Earth, adding their gravities together every 14 days (two weeks). Neap tides are extra-low, when the Sun and Moon are at right angles, so their pulling strengths partly cancel each other out. A neap tide occurs seven days after a spring tide.

▼ At new Moon and full Moon, the Sun, Moon and Earth are in a straight line, causing spring tides. At the first and last quarters of the Moon, the Sun and Moon are not aligned, so neap tides occur.

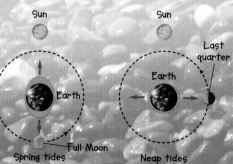

Sun

New Moon

Earth

Spring tides

Sun

First quarter

Earth

Neap tides

Sun

Earth

Full Moon

Spring tides

Sun

Last quarter

Earth

Neap tides

(4) Splash zone has lichens, which receive wave spray

(3) Upper intertidal zone is exposed to air most of the time – there are green wrack seaweeds and limpets

(2) Mid intertidal zone is submerged half of the time – there are mussels, barnacles, hermit crabs and brown seaweeds

(1) Lower intertidal zone is usually underwater – there are anemones, starfish, fish and red seaweeds

16 Tides produce 'zones' along seashores, from the high tide zone to the low tide zone. Different seaweeds and animals are adapted to each zone.

17 Ocean currents affect the seashore. A current flowing towards the shore can bring particles of sediment to add to the land. A current flowing away sweeps sediment out to sea. Currents also alter the direction and power of waves.

▲ The amount of time underwater determines which animals and plants live along a rocky shore.

18 If a wind blows waves at an angle onto a beach, each wave carries particles of sand upwards and sideways. When they recede, the particles roll back. Particles gradually zigzag along the shore – a process called longshore drift. Groynes built into the sea help to control it, so beaches don't wash away.

Seashore features

19 On a typical seashore, the struggle between land and sea produces various features. Much depends on the balance between the sea's wearing away of the land, and the formation of new land by particles settling in layers, known as sedimentation.

Stack

Headlan

Stump

Arch

Needle

Shingle spit

20 Hard or tough rocks can resist the sea's eroding power. They form tall cliffs and headlands that erode slowly. Softer rocks break apart more easily. The waves erode them at sea level, which is known as undercutting. The whole shore collapses as boulders tumble into the water.

Shingle or pebble beach

21 Waves and other shore-eroding forces may gradually cut through a headland, forming a cave. This can get worn through to form an arch of rock. When the arch collapses it leaves an isolated tall piece of rock, called a stack.

Groyne

▲ In this bay, waves and currents wash sediments with increasing power from right to left. Wall-like groynes or breakwaters lessen longshore drift.

Circular bay

Cliffs

Cave

Waves

22 **Waves and onshore currents flowing towards the land bring sediments to make low shores and mounds of sand, mud and silt.** These can lengthen to form long spits. During extra-high spring tides these sediments grow higher.

23 **Depending on winds and currents, a huge rounded scoop may be carved along the seashore to form a bay.** In sheltered parts of the bay, particles of sand gather to form a beach. As the bay gets more curved, it can break through the land behind to leave an island.

River →

Delta

Mudflats (bare mud near delta)

Saltmarsh (with plants)

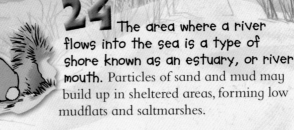

24 **The area where a river flows into the sea is a type of shore known as an estuary, or river mouth.** Particles of sand and mud may build up in sheltered areas, forming low mudflats and saltmarshes.

Sandy beach

17

Coast to coast

25 A seashore's features and wildlife depend on its location. Seashores near the Poles are cold most of the year and the sea may freeze for months. Almost no life can survive there.

◀ Antarctic coasts are mostly floating sheets and lumps of ice. Crabeater seals rest at the ice edge after feeding in the almost freezing water.

26 Some cold seashores have no land. Glaciers and ice shelves spread outwards, so the sea meets ice, not land. The edge of the ice may have smooth slopes and platforms cut by the waves. Jagged chunks of ice crack off and fall into the water as floating icebergs.

▼ Tropical seashores include coral reefs, like this one near Komodo Island, Southeast Asia, with huge biodiversity (range of living things).

27 In tropical regions around the middle of the Earth, seashore conditions are very different. It is warm for most of the year and many forms of life flourish, including seaweeds, fish, crabs, prawns, starfish and corals.

28 Exposure to wind is a powerful factor in the shaping of a shoreline. A windward seashore is exposed to strong prevailing winds. The winds make waves that hit the shore hard, sending salty spray to great heights. This type of shore has very different animals and plants from a leeward seashore, which is sheltered from the main winds.

29 Yearly seasons have an effect on seashores and their wildlife. Usually there is rough weather in winter, with winds and storms that increase land erosion. Some wildlife moves away from the shore in winter – birds fly inland while lobsters and fish move into deeper water.

30 The slope of the sea bed at the shore is very important, affecting the size and number of waves. A sea bed with a very shallow slope tends to produce smaller waves. A steep slope up to the beach gives bigger waves that erode the land faster, but are good for surfing!

LET'S SURF!

You will need:
sink or bathtub   water   tray

Put 10 centimetres of water into the sink or bathtub. Hold the tray at one end, at an angle so that part of it slopes into the water like a beach. Swish your other hand in the water to make waves hit the 'beach'. How does altering the tray's angle from low to high affect the waves?

▲ A big winter storm, such as this one in Sussex, UK, can smash even the strongest sea defences, which have to be repaired regularly.

Saltmarshes and mudflats

Sea thrift (sea pink) likes drier areas of marsh

Common cordgrass helps bind loose mud

Glasswort has fleshy leaves that store water

Sea aster flowers in late summer

▲ Saltmarsh plants have to endure harsh conditions, as they are exposed to both salt water and freshwater.

31 On a sheltered seashore, small particles of sediment collect. This happens around the mouths of rivers (estuaries). As the river's water speed slows, its floating particles sink to the bottom.

32 Saltmarshes have partly dry areas. They are rarely fully submerged, perhaps only with salty water at spring tides, or with freshwater if a nearby river floods.

▶ Many wading birds feed by probing into mud for small worms and shellfish.

Redshank

Curlew

33 Saltmarsh plants include glasswort, sea purslane, sea aster, sea lavender, sea thrift and red fescue. These plants are food for small creatures such as worms and insects, which are eaten by birds such as rails, curlews, herons and egrets.

34 Mudflats are usually lower and wetter than saltmarshes, as every high tide washes over them. Plants find it difficult to take root in these conditions, but a few, such as rice grass, cordgrass and eel grass, manage. Cordgrass grows in the wetter regions of saltmarshes around the world. It has glands to get rid of unwanted salt taken in from sea water.

35 Most mudflat animal life is under the surface. There are burrowing animals such as ragworms, mud shrimps and ghost crabs, and shelled creatures such as spireshells, towershells, cockles and various types of clams. Birds, especially waders such as godwits, knots and snipes, fly in at low tide to probe for these creatures.

Soft-shell clams like muddy shores best

Laver spireshells are also called mudsnails

Towershells feed in both sand and silt

Common cockles filter sea water for food

▲ Shelled animals with two shell halves are called bivalves. Spiral ones are types of sea-snails.

▼ Each year, summer plants grow into the calm waters of saltmarshes, spreading their greenery into the channels. However autumn storms soon wash them away.

I DON'T BELIEVE IT!

In some mudflats, the numbers of small shellfish, called spireshells, are greater than 50,000 in just one square metre!

Sandy beaches

36 Sandy shores need gentle winds, waves and currents that are still strong enough to wash away silt and mud. Just above high tide, any rain quickly drains away between the grains of sand, so it is too dry for land plants to grow. Below this, the grains move with wind, waves and tides, so few sea plants can grow there either.

37 Most sandy shore life is under the surface. Animals hide under the sand while the tide is out. As it rises, it brings with it tiny plants and animals, known as plankton, and bits of dead plants and creatures. Shrimps, lugworms, clams, tellins, scallops and heart urchins burrow through the sand or filter the water to feed.

38 Small sandy shore animals are meals for bigger predators that follow the tide, including cuttlefish, octopus and fish such as sea bass and flatfish. The giant sea bass of North Pacific shores grows to more than 2 metres long and weighs 250 kilograms.

▼ As the tide comes in, creatures hidden in the sand come out and start to feed – but predators are ready to eat them.

Jellyfish
may get washed up onto the beach and stranded

Cuttlefish
grab prey with their tentacles

Sand eels
feed on the bottom

Flatfish
have colours similar to the sea bed

Common shrimps
half-hide in burrows

▼ Fencing helps to keep sand dunes still, so grasses can start to grow.

39 As high tide retreats, it leaves a ribbon of washed-up debris along a beach, called the **strandline**. Animals including gulls, foxes, otters and lizards scavenge here for food, such as dead fish and crabs.

40 On some sandy shores, onshore winds blow the sand grains up the beach towards the land. Mounds, ridges and hills form seashore habitats called sand dunes. Marram grass can survive the wind and dryness, and its roots stop the grains blowing away, stabilizing the dunes.

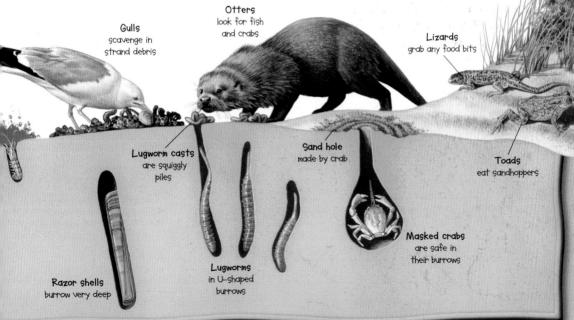

Gulls
scavenge in
strand debris

Otters
look for fish
and crabs

Lizards
grab any food bits

Lugworm casts
are squiggly
piles

Sand hole
made by crab

Toads
eat sandhoppers

Razor shells
burrow very deep

Lugworms
in U-shaped
burrows

Masked crabs
are safe in
their burrows

23

Mangrove swamps

41 Mangrove swamps are unusual shore habitats. They occur in the tropics where wind, waves and currents are weak, allowing mud to collect. The mud has no tiny air pockets, which land plants need to take oxygen from.

◄ Shoreline mangroves, here in East Africa, form a thick tangle where no other plants grow. These mangrove trees have stilt roots.

42 Mangrove trees use their unusual roots to get oxygen from the air. Some have stilt or prop roots, which hold the tree above the mud and water so it can take in oxygen through tiny holes in its bark. Others have aerial roots covered with tiny holes that poke above the mud into the air.

▼ Black mangroves, like these in Florida, USA, have aerial roots covered with tiny holes that poke above the mud into the air.

43 **Mangrove swamps teem with wildlife.** The biggest creatures include dugongs and manatees (large marine mammals) that eat the fallen leaves, flowers and fruits of mangrove trees. Fish and turtles swim among the roots, while mangrove and fiddler crabs burrow in the mud or climb the roots.

▲ Mangrove roots, stems and seaweeds form an underwater jungle where small predators, such as this lemon shark pup, hunt for victims.

44 **Roosting birds, land crabs, mangrove snakes and fishing cats live in mangroves.** In South and Southeast Asia, tigers slink between the trees looking for prey. One of the strangest inhabitants is the proboscis monkey. The male has a long, floppy nose, which can be up to 8 centimetres in length.

Male proboscis monkey

Female proboscis monkey

▶ Proboscis monkeys eat mainly mangrove leaves and fruits, and they are excellent swimmers.

Baby proboscis monkey

Shingle and pebbles

45 One of the harshest seashore habitats is the shingle, pebble or gravel beach. Fairly strong winds, waves and currents wash away smaller particles, such as silt and sand, leaving behind lumps of rock and stone. Sand or mud may collect over time, but a strong storm's crashing waves wash them away.

◄ On this New Zealand shingle beach, a storm has washed away some of the smaller pebbles to leave a line of larger cobbles, which protect the shingle higher up.

HIDDEN EGGS

You will need:
smooth, rounded pebbles   tray
watercolour paints and brush
three hen's eggs

Lay out the pebbles on the tray and look at their colours and patterns. Paint the hen's eggs to match the pebbles. Place the eggs among the pebbles. Are they so well camouflaged that your friends can't spot them?

46 Waves roll shingle and pebbles around, wearing away their sharp edges and making them smooth and rounded. Plants are in danger of being crushed by the waves, but oysterplant, sea kale and sea blite gain a roothold. Lichens, combinations of fungi or moulds, and simple plants known as algae, coat the stones.

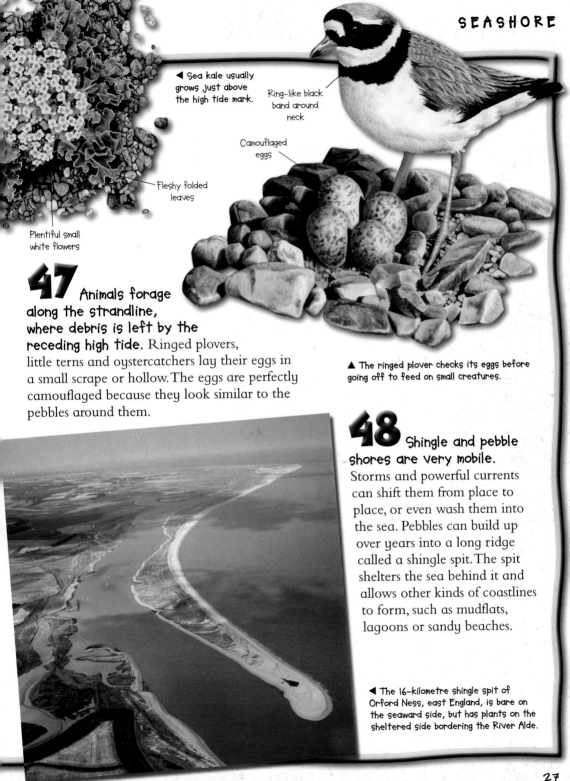

◀ Sea kale usually grows just above the high tide mark.

Ring-like black band around neck

Camouflaged eggs

Fleshy folded leaves

Plentiful small white flowers

47 Animals forage along the strandline, where debris is left by the receding high tide. Ringed plovers, little terns and oystercatchers lay their eggs in a small scrape or hollow. The eggs are perfectly camouflaged because they look similar to the pebbles around them.

▲ The ringed plover checks its eggs before going off to feed on small creatures.

48 Shingle and pebble shores are very mobile. Storms and powerful currents can shift them from place to place, or even wash them into the sea. Pebbles can build up over years into a long ridge called a shingle spit. The spit shelters the sea behind it and allows other kinds of coastlines to form, such as mudflats, lagoons or sandy beaches.

◀ The 16-kilometre shingle spit of Orford Ness, east England, is bare on the seaward side, but has plants on the sheltered side bordering the River Alde.

Estuaries and lagoons

▲ This maze of channels and sandbanks at the mouth of Australia's Murray River change over months and years, especially during winter storms.

49 An estuary is the end of a river at the coast, where it flows into the sea. The river might emerge through a narrow gap. Or it can gradually widen as it approaches the sea, so that at the shore it is so wide you cannot see from one side to the other.

50 The river water slows down as it flows into the sea and loses its movement energy. As this happens, its sediment particles settle out in order of size. This is known as sediment sorting or grading. As particles settle to the bottom, they may form a spreading area in the river mouth called a delta.

51 Estuaries are halfway habitats, with freshwater towards the river and salt water towards the sea. There is an ever-changing mixture inbetween due to tides, currents and rainfall. This partly salty water is known as brackish.

▶ Grizzly bears dig up tasty shellfish on an estuary beach in Canada.

QUIZ

Match these seashore visitors to their regions.
1. Leatherback turtle
2. Walrus
3. Adélie penguin
A. All warm and cool seas
B. Antarctic coasts
C. Arctic coasts

Answers:
1A 2C 3B

▲ Terns flock down to rest overnight on a remote beach before continuing their migration.

61 Visiting birds use seashores as resting places on their long yearly journeys (migrations). Some move to the coast for winter, when inland waters freeze. Migrants include waders or shorebirds such as dunlins, sandpipers, godwits and curlews. Wildfowl such as ducks, geese and swans also stop over on migration or overwinter on the shore.

▶ After laying about 150 eggs into the hole she dug, this female green turtle pushes sand on top to close the hole before returning to the water.

62 Among the rarest shore visitors is the sea turtle. The female hauls herself up the beach under cover of darkness, scoops a large hole with her flippers, lays her eggs in it, covers them and lumbers back to the sea. Weeks later the baby turtles hatch and dig their way to the surface. Then it's a race to the sea – many will be eaten by gathering predators on the way.

33

Above the seashore

63 **The skies above many seashores are busy with all kinds of flying animals.** Several kinds of birds rest or nest along the shore, flying out to sea or inland to feed.

◄ Different kinds of birds tend to perch and nest at different heights along the cliffs.

64 **Coastal cliffs are safe nesting places for many different seabirds.** It is difficult for predators, such as foxes, lizards or snakes, to reach the birds' eggs and chicks on steep rocky ledges. Cliff-nesters include fulmars, puffins, Manx shearwaters and gannets.

KEY

1. Great black-backed gull
2. Lesser black-backed gull
3. Herring gull
4. Rock dove
5. Chough
6. Puffin
7. Guillemot
8. Razorbill
9. Rock pipit
10. Fulmar
11. Kittiwake
12. Black guillemot

▲ In the past being a lighthouse–keeper was a vital but lonely job, with weeks alone tending the lamp and its machinery. Today most lighthouses, such as Fanad Head in north–west Ireland, are electric and mostly automatic.

75 For centuries fire beacons, lanterns, lighthouses and lightships have warned boats and ships about dangerous shores. Hazards include running aground on a sandbank or hitting rocks just under the surface. Each lighthouse flashes at a different time interval so sailors can identify it.

▼ The stonefish's fin spines can jab deadly venom into the skin.

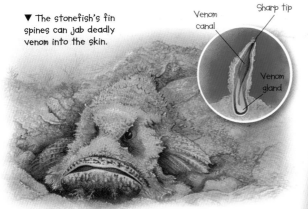

Venom canal

Sharp tip

Venom gland

▼ Fire coral is named after the burning pain it causes if touched.

76 Even just walking along a shore or paddling in shallow water can be dangerous, especially in tropical regions. There may be poisonous animals such as jellyfish, weeverfish, stonefish and shellfish known as coneshells, all of which have stings that can kill.

People and seashores

77 People have lived along seashores and coastlines for thousands of years. Settlers could hunt and gather food from the sea. They could travel by boat along the coast, up rivers to inland areas and across the sea to other regions. These boats carried raw materials, food and goods for trading.

78 Foods from the seashore include fish, octopus, crabs and lobsters caught with nets, spears or hooks and lines. Shellfish such as cockles, mussels, scallops, limpets and winkles are gathered by hand. Seaweeds can be harvested for food or to obtain chemicals used in many processes from dyeing textiles to glass-making.

79 Seashores are important in traditional arts, crafts and religions. Driftwood is carved into fantastic shapes, seashells are collected for their beauty, and necklaces made of sharks' teeth supposedly give strength to the wearer. Gods and spirits from the sea feature in many religions, faiths and customs, such as Kauhuhu the shark god of Hawaii.

▼ Sri Lankan fishermen perch on poles and watch for fish passing below as the tide changes.

▲ Lights never go out in Hong Kong harbour, one of the world's busiest seaports.

▼ More than 150,000 troops landed on Normandy beaches in France on D-Day, 6 June, 1944.

80 In recent times, large areas of coastal land in places such as the Netherlands, India, Bangladesh and southern USA have been made into rich farmlands. Sea walls and other defences keep the waves at bay. Reclaimed land is used for factories and industry, dwellings (as in Venice and Singapore), and airport runways (as in Sydney, Singapore and Hong Kong).

▼ Holiday developments completely destroy natural coasts, with increased travel by air and sea as tourists come and go.

81 Seashores have featured in empires and battles through the ages. Seafaring and trading centres, such as Constantinople (now Istanbul), Venice and London, were once hubs of great empires. Castles and forts keep out seaborne invaders. World War II's D-Day seaborne invasion of France's Normandy coastline in 1944 was the largest military event in history.

Seaside adventures

82 In modern times, seashores have become places for fun, leisure and adventure. People relax, sunbathe, play games and sports, and view buildings and monuments. In many countries, more than half of all tourism business is along coasts.

▲ Scuba-divers should 'take nothing but photographs and memories', leaving wildlife completely untouched.

▼ Adding just the right amount of water makes the sand firm for sculpting.

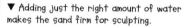

83 Fun activities at the seashore include swimming, snorkelling, scuba-diving, kite-flying and building sandcastles. People also paint, draw and photograph beautiful scenes of the waves, shore, sky and Sun. Many seaside resorts have sand sculpture competitions, where contestants produce amazing shapes from just sand and water.

94 Modern shore fishing and food harvesting does immense damage. Powerful boats with huge nets scour and scrape up life from the water and sea bed, leaving them empty. People fish with dynamite and poisonous chemicals. Unique habitats are destroyed and will take years to recover.

▲ Plastic nets and lines do not rot away naturally. They may trap animals, such as this green turtle, for months.

95 Global warming and climate change are looming problems for the whole Earth — especially seashores. Sea levels will rise, altering the shapes of coasts, wiping out natural shore habitats and man-made ones, and flooding low-lying land beyond, from wild areas to cities and rich farmland.

96 With global warming and climate change, more extreme weather may come along coasts. Hurricanes, typhoons and other storms could happen more often, causing destruction along the shores. Today's coastal flood defences, such as sea walls and estuary barriers, will be overwhelmed.

▼ Recycled materials can be used as sea walls to protect against rising sea levels — but they only last a few years.

SOS – Save our seashores

97 Seashores need our protection and conservation in many ways. Each shore is a unique habitat, and once gone, it may never return. With problems such as pollution coming from both the land and the sea, seashores are stuck in the middle and need extra care.

▼ Whales sometimes get stranded on beaches, perhaps because they are ill from pollution. Efforts to save them do not always succeed.

QUIZ

Match these animals to their favourite places.
1. Hermit crab 2. Seagull
3. Shore crab
A. Rockpool
B. Empty whelk shell
C. Seaside rubbish bin

Answers:
1B (to live in) 2C (for food) 3A (to hide in)

98 One way to conserve seashores is to make them protected nature reserves, wildlife parks or heritage sites. The area might be protected land that extends to the sea or a marine park that extends to the land. The world's biggest such park, at 360,000 square kilometres, is the Pacific's Papahānaumokuākea Marine National Monument. It includes the northwestern Hawaiian islands and the seas around.

99 You can help to protect seashores by supporting wildlife and conservation organizations, from huge international charities to smaller local ones. In the UK, contact your county-based Wildlife Trust and ask about seashore projects that might need help.

▲ Scientists travel to remote beaches to study wildlife, such as these walruses, and to find out how their seashore habitats are changing.

100 You can even help seashores on your own!

❁ Don't drop litter or leave rubbish along the shore, and ask others not to either.

❁ Encourage people to look after their seashores.

❁ Join an organized beach litter-pick or shore clean-up.

❁ Don't buy souvenirs that might have come from living wildlife, such as dried seahorses and starfish.

❁ Tell someone in authority (police, lifeguard, coastguard) if you come across an injured or stranded animal — but do not touch it.

Rainforests of the sea

101 Beautiful coral reefs lie beneath the sparkling surfaces of sapphire-blue seas. Although they only take up a tiny amount of space in the world's oceans, coral reefs contain more than one-quarter of all types of sea creatures and are home to billions of animals and plants. Coral reefs are among the Earth's most precious places but they are in grave danger of disappearing forever.

▲▶ Hawaiian corals (1) have grown on old lava that has cooled and turned to stone (2).

153 Volcanoes began to erupt in this area around 70 million years ago, and they are still active today. As lava cooled and turned to stone, corals began to grow on their edges. The first polyps must have arrived as free-swimming planulas, probably from other Pacific coral reefs.

◀ Green turtles lay their eggs on Hawaiian beaches because the reefs protect them from storms and waves.

154 The islanders of Hawaii set up a marine park in 1967, to protect the reef ecosystem. In 1956 an enormous channel, more than 60 metres wide, was blasted into the coral using dynamite to make way for a new telephone cable. The coral is now protected by law.

155 Around 10,000 endangered humpback whales visit Hawaii every year. They arrive at the warm tropical waters in the winter, after swimming all the way from their feeding grounds in Alaska. While in Hawaii, the whales give birth to their young, and care for them. They can be seen swimming, playing and even battling with one another around the coral reefs.

◀ A bobtail squid can produce light in its belly, which helps it hunt at night. The light is produced by bacteria that live on the squid.

A carnival of colour

156 Some animals stay on the sea floor, or hide in cracks in the coral reef, but others dart, dive and dazzle their way through the clear waters. Coral reef animals often use the colours of their shells or skins to help them lurk unseen in the shadows, or to warn other animals to stay away. When an animal uses colour to hide, it is said to be camouflaged.

157 Coral fish come in beautiful patterns and brilliant colours. Good looks are important for their survival – red colours appear dark in water, stripes provide camouflage and spots can confuse predators. Blue and yellow fish look bright to us, but they are hidden on the reef. The way sunlight is reflected off coral reefs affects the appearance of blues and yellows, making them blend in with the background.

▲▼ Coral fish come in many different colours and patterns such as the coral trout (top), regal angelfish (middle) and blue tang fish (below).

158 Squid and cuttlefish create flashes of colour. These soft-bodied molluscs can change their colours in an instant to hide or attract prey towards them. They can produce skin colours of red, yellow, orange, brown and black – and can even create patterns, such as zebra stripes, on their skin.

◀ Sea slugs are brightly coloured to warn predators that they are very poisonous.

159 Land slugs are slimy and often dull in colour, but coral reef slugs are bizarre, beautiful animals. Sea slugs, also called nudibranchs, don't have shells, but they do have soft, feathery gills on their backs, which help them to breathe in water. Some nudibranchs are small, but the largest ones can grow to 30 centimetres long.

160 The stripes, spines and bright colours of a lionfish spell danger to other coral creatures. These ocean fish hunt other fish, shrimp and sea anemones. When they are threatened they react with lightning speed. Lionfish have spines on their bodies that carry deadly venom, which they raise and plunge into a predator's flesh.

▼ Lionfish hide among rocks in the daytime, and only come out at night to hunt for food. They have been known to threaten divers.

GO FISH!

Choose your favourite colourful coral fish from this book and copy it onto a large piece of paper or card. Use different materials, such as paints, tissue paper, buttons and foil to show the colours and patterns.

75

On the attack

161 **Animals need energy to survive, and they get that energy from food.** Some reef animals graze on seaweeds and corals, but others hunt and kill to feed. Hunting animals are called predators, and their victims are called prey.

▶ When sharks, such as these lemon sharks, sense blood or food they move with speed to attack their prey.

162 **Some coral sharks aren't aggressive and divers can feed them by hand.** Bull sharks are not so relaxed around humans. They have been known to attack divers and swimmers around reefs. Sharks are drawn to coral reefs because of the thousands of fish on the reef but finding prey is not always easy when there are so many good hiding places.

163 **Cone shells look harmless, but their appearance is deceptive.** These sea snails crawl around reefs looking for prey such as worms, molluscs and fish. They fire venom-filled darts to paralyze their prey. The dart remains attached to the cone shell, so it can draw its victim back to its body and devour it.

◀ This small animal cannot protect itself from an attack by a deadly cone shell.

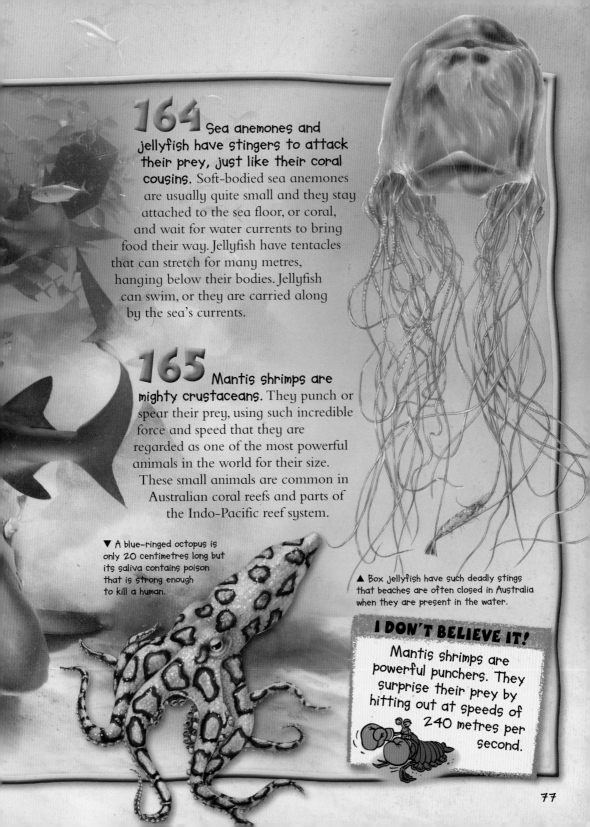

164 Sea anemones and jellyfish have stingers to attack their prey, just like their coral cousins. Soft-bodied sea anemones are usually quite small and they stay attached to the sea floor, or coral, and wait for water currents to bring food their way. Jellyfish have tentacles that can stretch for many metres, hanging below their bodies. Jellyfish can swim, or they are carried along by the sea's currents.

165 Mantis shrimps are mighty crustaceans. They punch or spear their prey, using such incredible force and speed that they are regarded as one of the most powerful animals in the world for their size. These small animals are common in Australian coral reefs and parts of the Indo-Pacific reef system.

▼ A blue-ringed octopus is only 20 centimetres long but its saliva contains poison that is strong enough to kill a human.

▲ Box jellyfish have such deadly stings that beaches are often closed in Australia when they are present in the water.

I DON'T BELIEVE IT!

Mantis shrimps are powerful punchers. They surprise their prey by hitting out at speeds of 240 metres per second.

Living together

166 **The animals and plants that live on coral reefs need each other to survive.** The close relationship between some animals is known as 'symbiosis'. Sometimes these partnerships give benefits to both animals, but at other times one animal gains little.

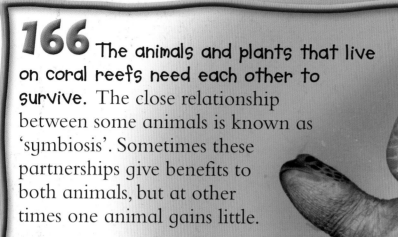

167 **Coral polyps and their zooxanthellae are best buddies.** Each zooxanthellae is made of just one cell. Like green plants, zooxanthellae make food using sunlight, water and carbon dioxide – a gas that is in the air. This process is called photosynthesis. The food they make is eaten by the polyps. Because they need sunlight to grow, zooxanthellae live inside a polyp's tentacles where light can reach them.

▼ Clownfish can hide among the stinging tentacles of a sea anemone without getting stung.

▲ Remora fish use other animals – such as this green turtle – to hitch a ride and find food.

I DON'T BELIEVE IT!
Boxer crabs use stinging sea anemones like boxing gloves. They wave them at any predators who get too close!

168 Coral fish dance to tell other reef animals that they are ready to get cleaning. Bluestreak cleaner wrasses feed on irritating parasites that attach themselves to other fishes' bodies, causing them harm. When they are hungry the wrasses dance to attract attention, and the bigger fish queue up to wait for their cleaning services.

▲ A moray eel patiently waits while a wrasse cleans its mouth.

169 Remoras are fish that hitch a ride on sharks, using specially adapted fins that work like sticky suckers. They get carried around the reef without having to spend any energy on swimming, but they may affect sharks' hunting ability by slowing them down. Remoras also latch on to dolphins and turtles.

170 Giant clams also have best buddies that they rely on to survive. These molluscs can grow up to 1.5 metres long and can live for more than 70 years. Zooxanthellae live on the fringes of these animals' enormous shells and provide the clams with nutrients. The clams and the algae need each other to survive, just like coral polyps and their algae.

▼ Hermit crabs depend on other shelled animals for their homes. They find empty shells and move in.

Night on the reef

171 As the Sun sets over the ocean, coral reefs change. Polyps emerge from their cups and unfurl their tentacles, producing a range of colours and movements. Creatures that were active in daylight rest in dark crevices, while others emerge to feed in the dark.

172 Coral animals that come out at night are described as nocturnal. They often have senses that help them to detect movement, light, sound and chemicals in the inky-blue seas. Octopuses have superb night vision and long tentacles that they use to probe cracks in the reef, searching for food.

◄ Corals are nocturnal and are most active at night.

173 Coral reef spiny lobsters march through the night. At the end of the summer 100,000 of them set off on a long journey. Walking in single file towards deeper, darker water, they can travel up to 50 kilometres every night to reach their breeding grounds.

▼ A Christmas tree worm buries its body deep inside a coral. Only its two feeding tentacles, which look like trees, are visible.

184

Scientists have been examining coral reefs for more than 300 years. There are many research centres and universities near large coral reefs, so scientists can collect information and learn about the reefs over many years. There are even underwater research laboratories, where scientists can study reefs close up for days at a time.

▼ Divers explore old reefs, but they also visit places where new reefs are forming on shipwrecks, to understand how they develop.

185

Exploring reefs is fascinating, but it can be dangerous too. Curious blacktip reef sharks may give a diver a warning nip, but a sting from a box jellyfish can be deadly. There are also poisonous sea snakes, octopuses, shellfish and fish.

Natural coral killers

186 **Some fish not only live on a reef, they eat it too.** There are more than 130 types of fish, known as corallivores, that feed on corals. They eat the slimy mucus made by polyps, the polyps themselves and even their stony cups. They like eating polyps during their breeding season because they are full of juicy, tasty eggs.

▲ Most coral-eating fish are butterfly fish. They have small mouths that can nibble at polyps and their eggs.

▼ Parrotfish change their appearance throughout their lives – they change colour as they grow up!

187 **Reef-killing creatures have different eating habits around the world.** In some regions, the coral-eating fish remove so much of the reef that it does not appear to grow at all. Threadfin butterfly fish in the Indian Ocean munch through large amounts of coral, but those that live around the Great Barrier Reef never eat coral. Corallivores that live in Caribbean reefs can survive on other food, too.

188 **Parrotfish are dazzling in their appearance, but deadly in their lifestyle.** They dig at coral with their tough mouths, which are like beaks, and grind it up in their throats. This releases the zooxanthellae that are an important part of their diet. The stony parts of the coral pass through their bodies, coming out the other end as beautiful white sand.

The ocean zones

ARCTIC OCEAN

PACIFIC OCEAN

202 Oceans are enormous areas of water. They cover more than two-thirds of the Earth's surface. There are five oceans and they make up a giant ecosystem of creatures that depend on seawater to survive.

ARCTIC OCEAN

ATLANTIC OCEAN

PACIFIC OCEAN

PACIFIC OCEAN

INDIAN OCEAN

SOUTHERN OCEAN

ATLANTIC OCEAN

203 At their edges, oceans are shallow and teem with life. These places are called continental shelves. However continental shelves only take up 5 percent of the total area of the oceans. The shelves fall away into deep slopes and from there, the seabed stretches out as dark, enormous plains.

SOUTHERN OCEAN

INDIAN OCEAN

◄▲ There are five oceans. They are all connected and make up one giant mass of water.

► Scientists divide the ocean into five layers, or zones. Different types of animals live in the different zones.

Jellyfish

LIGHT ZONE 0–200 metres

TWILIGHT ZONE 200–1000 metres

DARK ZONE 1000–4000 metres

Sea lily

ABYSSAL ZONE 4000–6000 metres

Tube worms

HADAL ZONE 6000–10,000 metres

DELIGHT IN LIGHT

Find out about the wavelengths of white light. How many colours make up white light, and what are they? Find the answers by searching on the Internet with the keywords 'rainbow' and 'light'.

Eye

Beak

Arm

224 People have known about giant squid for hundreds of years.

The first one to be recorded was found in Iceland in 1639, and the stories and myths began. People feared that these creatures could sink ships or grab people on deck. When sperm whales were discovered with scars caused by giant squid suckers, people realized that these predators battle with large whales.

225 Giant squid are predators.

No one knows for sure how they live, but like other squid they probably hunt fish, octopuses and smaller squid. Their muscular tentacles are equipped with giant, toothed suckers that can grab hold of wriggly prey.

▶ The eye of a giant squid has a diameter bigger than a person's head.

The Dark Zone

226 Below 1000 metres absolutely no light can penetrate. So far from the Sun's rays, this habitat is intensely cold, and there is bone-crushing pressure from the enormous weight of water above. It is called the Dark Zone, and it extends to 4000 metres below the ocean's surface.

227 It snows in the Dark Zone! Billions of particles fall down towards the seabed, and this is called marine snow. This 'snow' is made up of droppings from animals above, and animals and plants that have died. Small flakes often collect together to become larger and heavier, drifting down up to 200 metres a day. Marine snow is an important source of food for billions of deep-sea creatures.

▲ Fierce-looking fangtooth fish can swim to depths of around 5000 metres, into the Abyssal Zone, when they follow their prey.

I DON'T BELIEVE IT!

The orange roughy lives in deep water where its colour appears black if any light reaches it. This is believed to be one of the longest living fish – one individual allegedly reached 149 years of age.

228 A fangtooth fish may have enormous teeth, but at only 15 centimetres in length, these fish are not as scary as they sound. Fangtooths have poor eyesight, and in the Dark Zone other senses are just as valuable. These fish can detect tiny movements in the surrounding water, which they follow to find their prey.

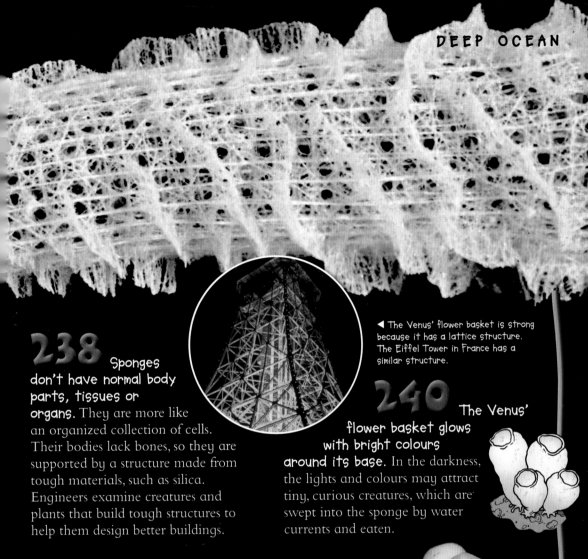

238 Sponges don't have normal body parts, tissues or organs. They are more like an organized collection of cells. Their bodies lack bones, so they are supported by a structure made from tough materials, such as silica. Engineers examine creatures and plants that build tough structures to help them design better buildings.

◀ The Venus' flower basket is strong because it has a lattice structure. The Eiffel Tower in France has a similar structure.

240 The Venus' flower basket glows with bright colours around its base. In the darkness, the lights and colours may attract tiny, curious creatures, which are swept into the sponge by water currents and eaten.

239 The Venus' flower basket builds its structure by 'gluing' together needles of silica, each no thicker than a human hair. The construction follows a beautiful pattern, which gives the sponge great strength to withstand the water pressure at depths of 5000 metres or more.

▶ Cloud sponges are another type of deep-living glass sponge. They can provide a safe living area for other small animals.

The Hadal Zone

241 The oceans plunge to depths greater than 6000 metres in only a few places, called trenches. This is called the Hadal Zone, named after the Greek word 'hades', which means 'unseen'. It's the perfect name for the most mysterious habitat on Earth.

Mariana Trench 11,034 metres
Tonga Trench 10,882 metres
Philippine Trench 10,540 metres
Kuril-Kamchatka Trench 10,500 metres
Kermadec Trench 10,047 metres
Bonin Trench 9994 metres
New Britain Trench 9940 metres
Izu Trench 9780 metres

Mount Everest 8850 metres

▲ Earth's largest mountain, Everest, could fit into eight of the world's deepest trenches.

242 The deepest of all trenches is the Mariana Trench in the Pacific Ocean, which plunges to 11,034 metres. It is 2550 kilometres long and about 70 kilometres wide. This trench was created when two massive plates in the Earth's crust collided millions of years ago.

243 Scientists know very little about animals that live in the Hadal Zone. Collecting live animals from this depth causes great problems because their bodies are suited to high water pressure. When they are brought to the surface the pressure drops, and they die.

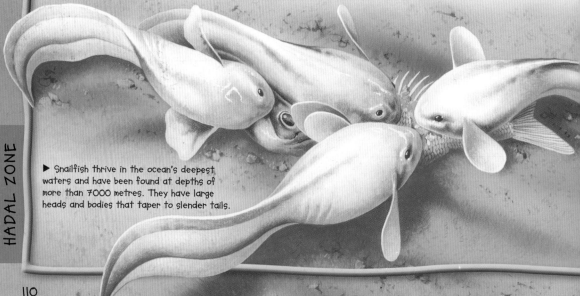

▶ Snailfish thrive in the ocean's deepest waters and have been found at depths of more than 7000 metres. They have large heads and bodies that taper to slender tails.

HADAL ZONE

254 Some hydrothermal vents do not support much life, other than microscopic creatures. Others support colonies of limpets, shrimps, starfish and tube worms, which survive without any sunlight. They are able to live and grow due to the minerals in the super-heated water from the vents.

▲ Hydrothermal vents known as 'white smokers' release cooler water and plumes of different minerals to black smokers.

255 Vent tube worms can grow to 2 metres long and they live without eating anything. Each worm is attached to the seabed and is protected by the tube it lives in. A red plume at the top collects seawater, which is rich in minerals. These minerals are passed to bacteria in the worm's body, and are then turned into nutrients.

6

7

Plume

Blood vessel

◄ Bacteria that live inside the tube worm turn the minerals into food, which the worm needs to survive.

Heart

Bacteria

Tube

UNDER PRESSURE

You will need:
milk carton   sticky tape

With an adult's help, make four holes on one side of an old milk carton, one above the other. Put sticky tape over the holes and fill the carton with water. Hold it over a bowl while you pull the tape off. Water will pour out fastest from the bottom hole because it has the most pressure on it.

Deep-sea coral

256 Tiny creatures called coral polyps build large reefs in the cold, deep ocean. Coral reefs are often found in warm, shallow waters, and they attract a wide variety of life. Cold-water reefs are not such varied habitats, but there may be more cold-water reefs than warm-water ones.

257 Coral polyps have tube-shaped bodies and tentacles around their mouths. All polyps feed by filtering food particles from the water, and they have thousands of tiny stingers to stun bigger prey.

Bubble gum coral

258 Coral polyps produce a hard substance called calcium carbonate, which forms a protective cup around them. Over time, the stony cups collect and grow into a reef, held together by a cement of sand, mud and other particles.

I DON'T BELIEVE IT!

Air pollution from carbon dioxide causes the oceans to become more acidic. This stops polyps, especially cold-water ones, from being able to grow their stony skeletons.

Flytrap anemone

Lophelia pertusa

Squat lobster

As a sperm whale dives, its ribs and lungs contract (shrink). They expand again when the whale surfaces.

The whale's heartbeat slows by half so less oxygen is needed.

The spermaceti organ is a huge mass of oil. It probably helps the whale to dive deep by changing its ability to float.

The nasal passages fill with cool water to help the whale sink.

▲ The sperm whale is adapted for diving in very deep water. It can stay underwater for up to 90 minutes while hunting for giant squid.

268 Seals, dolphins and whales are air-breathing mammals, but their bodies are adapted to life in water. The sperm whale can store oxygen in its blood and muscles, which allows it to descend to over 1000 metres to hunt. Its flexible ribcage allows the whale's lungs to shrink during a dive.

269 Super-speedy pilot whales are called 'cheetahs of the deep'. During the day, these predators swim at depths of around 300 metres, but at night they plunge to 1000 metres in search of prey. Pilot whales can plummet 9 metres a second at top swimming speed. They need to be fast to catch their prey of large squid, but also because they need to get back to the surface to breathe.

▼ Most marine worms have feathery gills that absorb oxygen from the water. However, some do not have gills and absorb oxygen through their skin.

270 Simple creatures do not have special body parts for breathing. They can absorb oxygen from the water directly through their skins. The amount of oxygen in the water falls from the surface to a depth of around 1000 metres, but it increases again at greater depths.

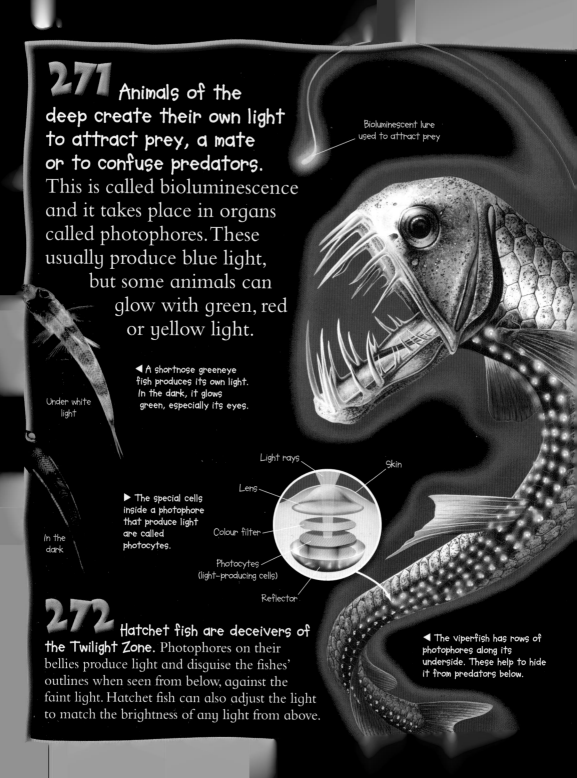

271 Animals of the deep create their own light to attract prey, a mate or to confuse predators. This is called bioluminescence and it takes place in organs called photophores. These usually produce blue light, but some animals can glow with green, red or yellow light.

Bioluminescent lure used to attract prey

◄ A shortnose greeneye fish produces its own light. In the dark, it glows green, especially its eyes.

Under white light

In the dark

► The special cells inside a photophore that produce light are called photocytes.

Light rays

Skin

Lens

Colour filter

Photocytes (light-producing cells)

Reflector

272 Hatchet fish are deceivers of the Twilight Zone. Photophores on their bellies produce light and disguise the fishes' outlines when seen from below, against the faint light. Hatchet fish can also adjust the light to match the brightness of any light from above.

◄ The viperfish has rows of photophores along its underside. These help to hide it from predators below.

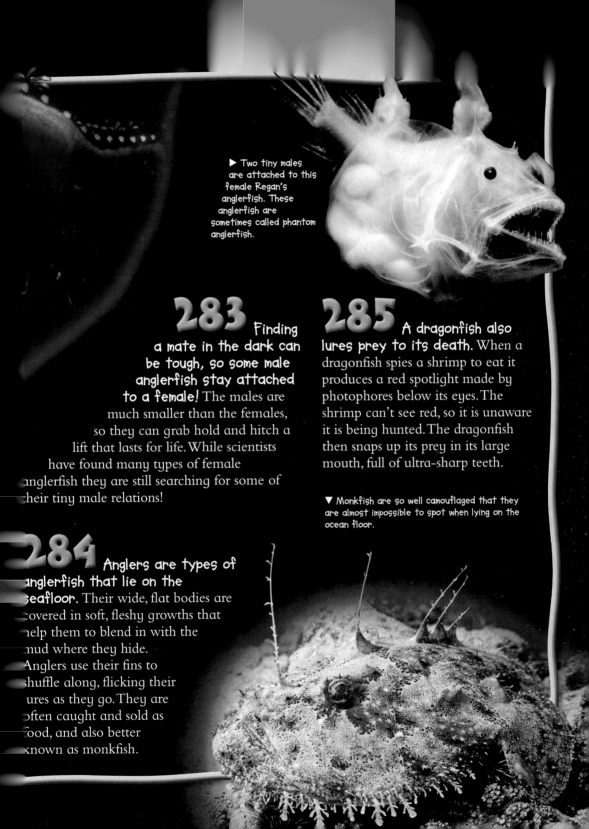

▶ Two tiny males are attached to this female Regan's anglerfish. These anglerfish are sometimes called phantom anglerfish.

283 Finding a mate in the dark can be tough, so some male anglerfish stay attached to a female! The males are much smaller than the females, so they can grab hold and hitch a lift that lasts for life. While scientists have found many types of female anglerfish they are still searching for some of their tiny male relations!

285 A dragonfish also lures prey to its death. When a dragonfish spies a shrimp to eat it produces a red spotlight made by photophores below its eyes. The shrimp can't see red, so it is unaware it is being hunted. The dragonfish then snaps up its prey in its large mouth, full of ultra-sharp teeth.

▼ Monkfish are so well camouflaged that they are almost impossible to spot when lying on the ocean floor.

284 Anglers are types of anglerfish that lie on the seafloor. Their wide, flat bodies are covered in soft, fleshy growths that help them to blend in with the mud where they hide. Anglers use their fins to shuffle along, flicking their lures as they go. They are often caught and sold as food, and also better known as monkfish.

Hide and seek

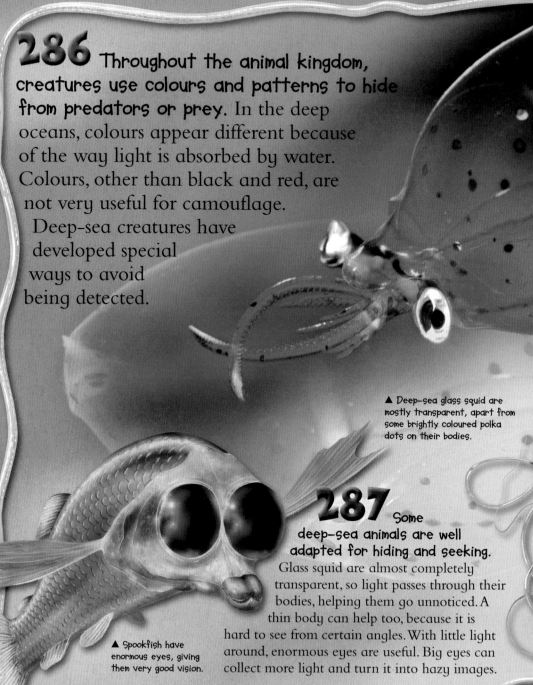

286 Throughout the animal kingdom, creatures use colours and patterns to hide from predators or prey. In the deep oceans, colours appear different because of the way light is absorbed by water. Colours, other than black and red, are not very useful for camouflage. Deep-sea creatures have developed special ways to avoid being detected.

▲ Deep-sea glass squid are mostly transparent, apart from some brightly coloured polka dots on their bodies.

▲ Spookfish have enormous eyes, giving them very good vision.

287 Some deep-sea animals are well adapted for hiding and seeking. Glass squid are almost completely transparent, so light passes through their bodies, helping them go unnoticed. A thin body can help too, because it is hard to see from certain angles. With little light around, enormous eyes are useful. Big eyes can collect more light and turn it into hazy images.

288 Silvery scales on a fish's back are perfect for reflecting light and confusing a predator. When shimmering scales are seen against dim rays of light in the Twilight Zone, the outline of a fish's body becomes less obvious, and it fades into the background or even disappears.

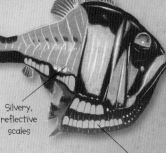

Silvery, reflective scales

Light-producing photophores

289 When there is no light, animals rely on senses other than sight. Many deep-sea animals can feel vibrations in the water. Shrimp have sensory organs all over their bodies, including their antennae, which can detect movements nearby. Many fish can also sense the small electrical fields generated by other living things.

▲ By using their photophores to produce light and their silvery scales to reflect light, hatchet fish become almost invisible to predators.

▶ The snipe eel's jaws curve away from each other so they never fully close.

290 Snipe eels have long, ribbon–like bodies, and jaws that look like a bird's bill. They live at depths of up to 1800 metres and can grown to 1.5 metres in length. As males mature their jaws shrink, but their nostrils grow longer. This probably improves their sense of smell and helps them to find females.

ODD ONE OUT
Which of these animals uses colour and pattern to scare other animals, rather than to hide?
Zebra Wasp Tiger
Leaf insect
Arctic fox

Answer:
Wasp

Searching the deep

▼ This timeline shows how technology has developed, improving ways of exploring the deep ocean.

1775 The *Turtle* was an early, one-man submarine

1837 The waterproof Siebe diving suit was developed

1872 HMS *Challenger* set sail for a four-year study of the deep ocean

1882 The USS *Albatross* continued this important research

1925 *Meteor* began mapping the seafloor

1934 William Beebe and Otis Barton used a bathysphere to make the first deep-ocean dive

Thruster

Oxygen supply

Boat cable

Pincer

▲ Newt Suits have joints, so divers can move their arms and legs.

291 **Early ocean explorers had to overcome many problems.** Divers needed a supply of air and to be able to cope with the water pressure. If divers ascend too quickly, the sudden change in pressure can cause the bends – a life-threatening sickness.

292 **The first diving suit was invented in the 1830s.** It was made of waterproof canvas and rubber, and allowed divers to descend to around 60 metres. About 40 years later a ship called the HMS *Challenger* explored the deeper oceans.

293 **Today's deep-diving suits are made of metal.** These Newt Suits allow divers to work at a depth of 300 metres. Suits have thrusters to help divers move underwater, communication systems to link to the boat at the surface, and video cameras.

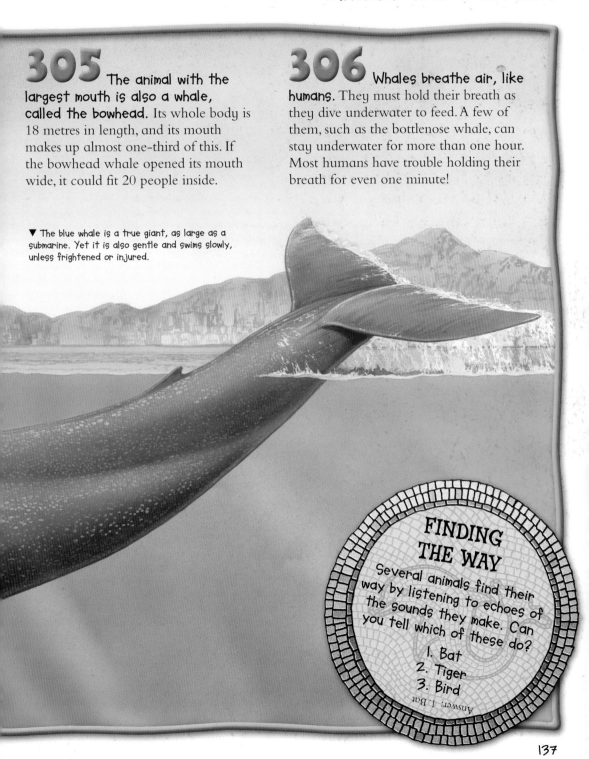

305

The animal with the largest mouth is also a whale, called the bowhead. Its whole body is 18 metres in length, and its mouth makes up almost one-third of this. If the bowhead whale opened its mouth wide, it could fit 20 people inside.

▼ The blue whale is a true giant, as large as a submarine. Yet it is also gentle and swims slowly, unless frightened or injured.

306

Whales breathe air, like humans. They must hold their breath as they dive underwater to feed. A few of them, such as the bottlenose whale, can stay underwater for more than one hour. Most humans have trouble holding their breath for even one minute!

FINDING THE WAY

Several animals find their way by listening to echoes of the sounds they make. Can you tell which of these do?

1. Bat
2. Tiger
3. Bird

Answer: 1. Bat

One big family

307 The mammal group of cetaceans is made up of about 80 kinds of whale, dolphin and porpoise. The whale group is divided into two main types – baleen whales and toothed whales.

308 Baleen whales are the largest members of the cetacean group and are often called great whales. They catch food with long strips in their mouths called baleen or whalebone. One example is the sei whale, which is about 16 metres in length and can reach a weight of 25 tonnes.

▲ The sperm whale is the biggest toothed whale. It only seems to have teeth in its lower jaw because those in its upper jaw can barely be seen.

CREATE A DOLPHIN!

You will need:
paper   coloured pens or pencils
Draw a dolphin outline and colour it any pattern you wish. You can name it after its colour, such as the pink-spotted dolphin. Or use your own name, like Amanda's dolphin.

309 Toothed whales catch prey with their sharp teeth. This subgroup includes sperm whales, beaked whales and pilot whales. One example is the beluga, also known as the white whale. It lives in the cold waters of the Arctic and can grow up to 5 metres in length. It is one of the noisiest whales, making clicks, squeaks and trills.

310
Another group is made up of beaked whales. These are medium-sized whales with long, beak-shaped mouths. There are about 20 kinds, but some are very rare and hardly ever seen. The shepherd's beaked whale, which is about 7 metres in length, has been seen fewer than 20 times.

311
There are six species of porpoise. They are usually quite small, at 2 metres or less in length. They have blunter, more rounded heads than dolphins. The finless porpoise, as its name suggests, has a smooth back with no fin.

◄ The finless porpoise, with its blunt 'beak' and bulging forehead, is one of the smallest cetaceans at about 1.5 metres in length.

▲ The dusky dolphin is very inquisitive and likes to swim and leap near boats, perhaps in the hope of being fed.

312
There are more than 35 kinds of dolphin. Most of them are 2 to 3 metres in length. They are fast swimmers and can often be seen leaping above the waves. The dusky dolphin is one of the highest leapers, twisting and somersaulting before it splashes back into the sea.

Inside whales and dolphins

313 **Whales, dolphins and porpoises are mammals, like humans.** They have the same parts inside their bodies as humans. These include bones to make up the skeleton, lots of muscles, a stomach to hold food, a heart to pump blood, and lungs to breathe air.

314 Most mammals have hair or fur, including humans. Whales, dolphins and porpoises are unusual because they have smooth, hairless skin to help them slip easily through the water. Only a few hairs, mainly bristles, can be found around the eyes, nose and mouth.

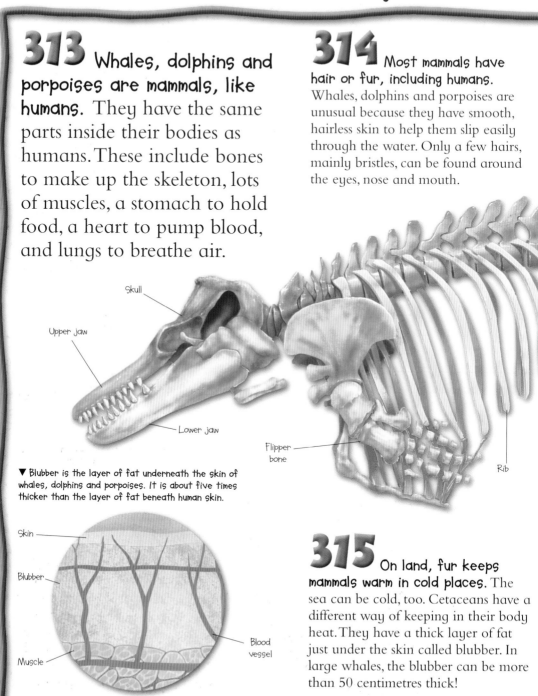

Skull

Upper jaw

Lower jaw

Flipper bone

Rib

▼ Blubber is the layer of fat underneath the skin of whales, dolphins and porpoises. It is about five times thicker than the layer of fat beneath human skin.

Skin

Blubber

Muscle

Blood vessel

315 On land, fur keeps mammals warm in cold places. The sea can be cold, too. Cetaceans have a different way of keeping in their body heat. They have a thick layer of fat just under the skin called blubber. In large whales, the blubber can be more than 50 centimetres thick!

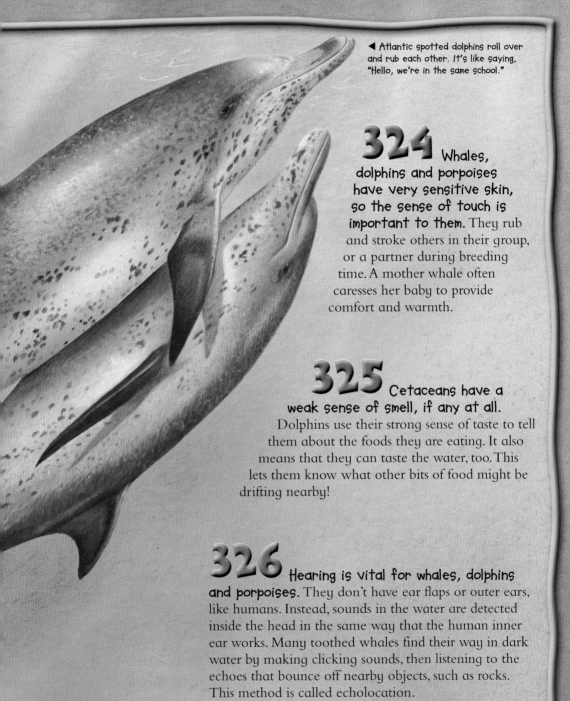

◄ Atlantic spotted dolphins roll over and rub each other. It's like saying, "Hello, we're in the same school."

324 Whales, dolphins and porpoises have very sensitive skin, so the sense of touch is important to them. They rub and stroke others in their group, or a partner during breeding time. A mother whale often caresses her baby to provide comfort and warmth.

325 Cetaceans have a weak sense of smell, if any at all. Dolphins use their strong sense of taste to tell them about the foods they are eating. It also means that they can taste the water, too. This lets them know what other bits of food might be drifting nearby!

326 Hearing is vital for whales, dolphins and porpoises. They don't have ear flaps or outer ears, like humans. Instead, sounds in the water are detected inside the head in the same way that the human inner ear works. Many toothed whales find their way in dark water by making clicking sounds, then listening to the echoes that bounce off nearby objects, such as rocks. This method is called echolocation.

Breathing and diving

327 **Whales, dolphins and porpoises breathe air in and out of their lungs.** They don't have gills to breathe underwater, like a fish, so they must hold their breath when diving. Air goes in and out of their body through the blowholes – small openings on top of the head, just in front of the eyes. They work like human nostrils, just in a different place on the head!

▲ As a whale breathes out, its 'blow' often looks like a steamy fountain of water. It can be seen far away across the ocean – and on a calm day, it can be heard from a distance, too.

328 **When a whale comes to the surface after a dive, it breathes out air hard and fast.** The moist air, mixed with slimy mucus from the whale's breathing passages, turns into water droplets. This makes the whale's breath look like a jet of steam or a fountain. It's called the 'blow'. All whales have 'blows' of different size and shape. This can help humans to identify them when they are hidden underwater.

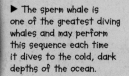

▶ The sperm whale is one of the greatest diving whales and may perform this sequence each time it dives to the cold, dark depths of the ocean.

1. The sperm whale surfaces and breathes in and out powerfully several times

2. It then straightens out its body and may disappear beneath the surface

▲ A giant squid tries to escape a sperm whale. The largest giant squid ever caught by a sperm whale was 12 metres in length.

329 Many cetaceans feed near the surface, so do not need to dive more than 50 metres down. The champion diver is the sperm whale. It can go down more than 3000 metres to hunt its prey of giant squid.

330 Most dolphins and porpoises dive and hold their breath for one or two minutes. Large whales can stay underwater for a longer period of time, perhaps for 15 to 20 minutes. The sperm whale can dive for more than two hours!

6. The sperm whale dives deep into the darkness of the ocean

3. The whale then reappears and begins to arch its back

4. By arching its back and tipping its head downwards, the whale prepares to dive

5. Its tail is lifted out of the water as it begins to dive

Fierce hunters

331 Dolphins, porpoises and toothed whales are active hunting carnivores. They eat meat – the flesh of sea creatures, especially fish and squid. Some of them crunch up hard-shelled crabs, shrimps and prawns, or shellfish, such as oysters and whelks.

332 A typical dolphin has 60 to 100 teeth. They are in pairs, left and right, in the upper and lower jaws. These teeth are not usually thin and sharp like fangs, but wide and cone-shaped. The teeth are the same shape all along the jaw, unlike the teeth of a cat, dog or human. This is the best design for catching their slippery food.

333 Beaked whales mainly eat squid. In some species, males have just two or four teeth, which look like tusks. Females have none at all. These whales suck in their prey and swallow it whole.

334 The sperm whale, has about 50 teeth in its lower jaw, which are about 20 centimetres in length. The teeth in its upper jaw are so tiny, they can barely be seen.

335 Most dolphins and porpoises must chase their speedy prey, quickly twisting and turning in the water, snapping at victims. Once a dolphin catches its prey, it flicks the fish back into its mouth, and swallows it whole. With a larger victim, the dolphin bites off a big chunk and swallows it. Whales, dolphins and porpoises hardly ever chew their food.

▲ Bottlenose dolphins swim around small fish that gather into a tight group called a 'bait-ball'. Then the dolphins dash into the bait-ball and try to grab the fish.

Sieving the sea

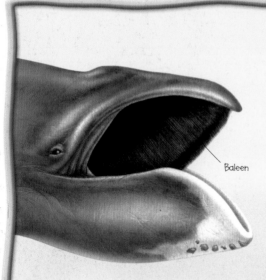

▲ The bowhead whale's baleen hangs like a huge curtain, big enough for ten people to hide behind.

Baleen

336 Great whales are also called baleen whales because of the baleen in their mouths. Baleen is sometimes called whalebone, but it is not bone. It's light, tough and springy, almost like plastic. It hangs down in long strips from the whale's upper jaw. The size and shape of the strips vary from one kind of whale to another.

337 Most baleen whales, such as the blue, fin and sei whales, cruise-feed. This means that they feed by swimming slowly through a swarm of shrimplike creatures called krill with their mouths open.

338 As a baleen whale feeds, it takes in a huge mouthful of water — enough to fill more than 100 bathtubs. This makes the skin around its throat expand like a balloon. The whale's food, such as krill, is in the water. The whale pushes the water out between the baleen plates. The baleen's bristles catch the krill like a giant filter. Then the whale licks off the krill and swallows them.

339

The humpback whale makes a 'bubble curtain'. It dives down, then swims up slowly in small circles as it breathes out. The bubbles created rise quickly and form a tube-shaped 'curtain' that keeps the krill or other food close together in one place as a 'bait-ball'. Then the humpback lunges into the bait-ball with its mouth wide open.

▶ Humpback whales feed by rising up through shoals of fish with their mouths open and throat skin bulging. They scoop up water, push it out through the baleen and eat the food left inside their mouths.

I DON'T BELIEVE IT!

In summer, the blue whale eats 4 tonnes of food in one day! That's about four million krill. In winter, it eats hardly anything for many weeks because food is scarce.

340

The grey whale often feeds on the shallow seabed. It swims on one side and drags its mouth through the mud. Then it pushes the water and mud out of its mouth. This traps food in its baleen, such as shellfish and shrimps. Its feeding method leaves deep grooves in the seabed, like a ploughed field.

Clicks, squeaks and squeals

341 **Many whales, dolphins and porpoises are noisy animals.** They make lots of different sounds, for various reasons. These sounds can travel long distances through the sea, so when underwater, divers can hear them. Some whale noises can be heard more than 100 kilometres away!

342 **Sounds are made by air moving around inside the breathing passages, and also inside the intestines and stomach.** In dolphins, sound waves are brought together, or focused, by the large fluid-filled lump inside the forehead called the melon. This makes sounds travel out from the front of the head in a narrow beam.

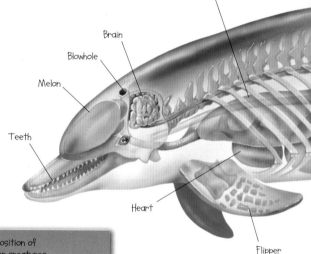

Lung

Brain

Blowhole

Melon

Teeth

Heart

Flipper

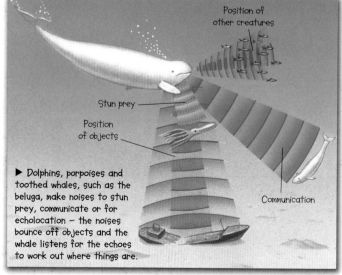

Position of other creatures

Stun prey

Position of objects

▶ Dolphins, porpoises and toothed whales, such as the beluga, make noises to stun prey, communicate or for echolocation – the noises bounce off objects and the whale listens for the echoes to work out where things are.

Communication

343 **Sounds are especially important for detecting objects by echolocation.** The dolphin detects the returning echoes of its own clicks. It can then work out the size and shape of objects nearby – whether a rock, coral, a shipwreck, an iceberg or a shoal of fish.

367

The harbour or common porpoise is familiar to sailors around the northern waters. It has the nickname 'puffing pig' because its blow is rarely seen, but can be heard as a series of loud, short puffs – like a mixture of a snort and a sneeze. It eats a wide range of food, including leftovers thrown from boats.

STRANDED!

You're at the beach and you see a stranded whale, do you...

A. Run away and keep quiet
B. Find an adult, and contact the police or coastguard
C. Sing the whale a song

Answer: B.

▼ When Dall's porpoise swims quickly through water, a long, narrow spray spurts along its back. It is known as the 'rooster's tail' due to its shape.

368

Dall's porpoise is the largest of the group, at about 2 metres in length and 200 kilograms in weight. It lives along the shores of the North Pacific Ocean. It's a fast and agile swimmer, dashing along at over 50 kilometres an hour. However, it rarely leaps above the surface of the water like other porpoises.

Getting together

369 Whales, dolphins and porpoises breed like most other mammals. A male and female get together and mate. The female becomes pregnant and a baby develops inside her womb. The baby is born through her birth canal, which is a small opening near her tail.

370 Breeding narwhals can be dangerous. This is because the males swipe and jab each other with their long 'tusks' to try and become partners for waiting females. The tusk is a very long left upper tooth that grows like a sword with a corkscrew pattern. Usually only the males have a tusk, which can be up to 3 metres in length.

◀ At breeding time male narwhals 'fence' with their tusks. They're competing for a female.

▼ In 1588, Spain sent an Armada (fleet of ships) to attack England, but it was scattered by English fireships (ships set on fire and sent towards enemies), and around half were wrecked in a storm. This painting is called *Defeat of the Spanish Armada*, and was painted by Philippe-Jacques de Loutherbourg in 1797.

How ships float – and sink

402 The Greek scientist Archimedes found out why things float over 2000 years ago. He jumped into his bath and noticed that when he did so, the water overflowed. He realized his body was pushing the water out. When ships float, they 'displace' water, in the same way.

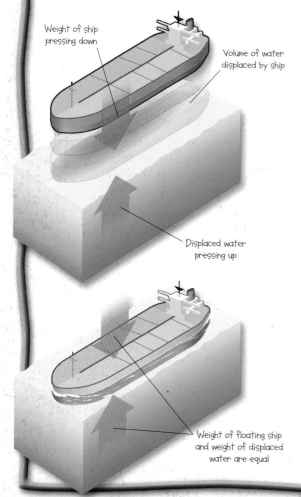

Weight of ship pressing down

Volume of water displaced by ship

Displaced water pressing up

Weight of floating ship and weight of displaced water are equal

◀ The water displaced by a floating ship pushes back with a powerful force equal to the ship's weight.

403 Archimedes discovered that water displaced by a ship pushes back on the ship with a force equal to its weight. This holds the ship up in the water. The density of a ship is also important. Density is the weight of an object measured along with its volume. If a ship or any object is less dense than water, it will float. If it is more dense than water, it will sink.

404 Ships are often made of materials such as iron or steel, which are denser than water. However, ships also contain a lot of air. Air is very light, and makes the ship much less dense than water.

MAKE A PENDANT

You will need:
clay   gold paint   paintbrush   ribbon

1. Shape a disk of clay 4 centimetres across and half a centimetre thick.

2. Press a ship design into the disk, and make a hole at the top.

3. Leave to dry, then paint with the gold paint and leave to dry again.

5. Thread the ribbon through the hole. Your pendant is ready to wear!

▶ Combining evidence from shipwrecks with images like this medieval seal allows archaeologists to work out what the Bremen Cog might have looked like over 600 years ago.

433 **One kind of pot that was found on the Pisa wreck is a mystery.** Called a 'spheroconus', it is shaped like a globe with a spout. It may have been used to store mercury – a poisonous medieval medicine – or water from Mecca, the Muslim holy city. Or it might have been a weapon to throw at enemy ships!

434 **Few medieval shipwrecks survive.** The wood, hemp fibre and canvas they were made of has rotted away. One of the best-preserved medieval wrecks is the Bremen Cog, from Germany. It was found in 1962, by dredgers (digging machines) widening a harbour entrance.

435 **The Bremen Cog was wrecked before it ever set sail.** Around 1380, floods swept it from a ship-builder's yard. After being stranded on a sandbank, it became covered with mud and silt. This stopped bacteria from rotting its timbers.

Chinese junks

436 Chinese junks were the biggest ocean-going sailing ships in the world. We know this from Chinese shipwrecks. In 1973, a wrecked junk was discovered near Quanzhou, south China. It was 34 metres in length and 11 metres in width and could carry 350 tonnes. It had three tall masts and was five times bigger than most European ships of its time.

437 Junks had special features that made them unlikely to sink. They had bulkheads (walls), which divided their hulls into compartments. Each compartment had a watertight cover and a drainage channel.

438 The Quanzhou junk was wrecked around 1275, probably in a typhoon (hurricane). It was blown onto rocks, a huge hole was smashed in its hull, and all the compartments filled with water. Accidents like this show that even the best-designed ships cannot always survive the very worst weather.

439 Lucky charms were hidden on junks for extra protection at sea. Divers exploring the Quanzhou wreck found seven bronze coins and a mirror. These represented the moon and the stars – traditional Chinese symbols of fair winds and good fortune.

QUIZ

1. How long was the Quanzhou wreck?

2. What is a typhoon?

3. Who travelled on junks?

Answers:
1. 34 metres in length
2. A hurricane 3. Merchants

440 Around 60 merchants sailed on the Quanzhou wreck. Each had his own cabin. They were travelling with precious cargoes from Africa and South Asia, including pepper, perfumes, tortoiseshell and seashells (which they used like coins). Other junks carried spices and fine pottery.

◄ A Chinese junk, similar to the Quanzhou junk, is blown across the sea by a violent typhoon. The sailors struggle to lower its sails to reduce its speed through the water. Waves surge around the hull, but its waterproof design helps it stay afloat, unless it is holed.

Tudor ship

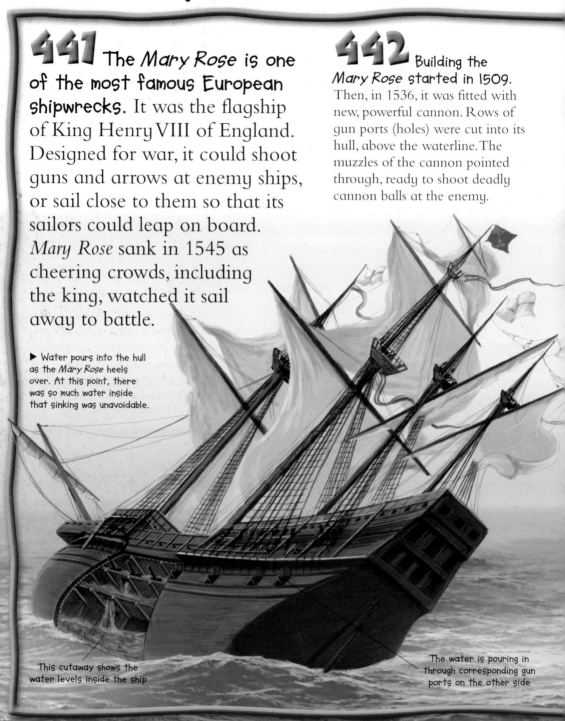

441 The *Mary Rose* is one of the most famous European shipwrecks. It was the flagship of King Henry VIII of England. Designed for war, it could shoot guns and arrows at enemy ships, or sail close to them so that its sailors could leap on board. *Mary Rose* sank in 1545 as cheering crowds, including the king, watched it sail away to battle.

▶ Water pours into the hull as the *Mary Rose* heels over. At this point, there was so much water inside that sinking was unavoidable.

442 Building the *Mary Rose* started in 1509. Then, in 1536, it was fitted with new, powerful cannon. Rows of gun ports (holes) were cut into its hull, above the waterline. The muzzles of the cannon pointed through, ready to shoot deadly cannon balls at the enemy.

This cutaway shows the water levels inside the ship

The water is pouring in through corresponding gun ports on the other side

▲ Slowly and very carefully, the wreck of the *Mary Rose* is lifted from the seabed on a massive metal cradle that has been specially made in exactly the same shape as the ship's hull.

443 The weight of people and guns on the upper decks made the *Mary Rose* unstable. Suddenly, it heeled (leaned over) to one side and water poured in through its gun ports. It could not right itself (return to an upright, balanced position), filled with water, and sank rapidly. The soldiers and sailors on board were trapped by nets meant to keep out enemies. Around 500 drowned.

444 The *Mary Rose* came to rest leaning on its starboard (right-hand) side. Its starboard decks and cabins sank unharmed into the soft mud of the seabed, close to Portsmouth, southern England. Year by year, layers of silt covered the wreck, hiding it completely. The *Mary Rose* became a secret Tudor time capsule.

445 Investigators have tried to explore the *Mary Rose* wreck several times. Soon after it sank, Italian experts tried to find its valuable cannon. Between 1836 and 1840, divers dropped explosives near the wreck to uncover it. Archaeologists surveyed the wreck in 1967, then began to excavate it in 1979. In 1982, the remains of the *Mary Rose* were lifted to the surface. Today, they are displayed in a museum.

I DON'T BELIEVE IT!

In just four years, from 1979 to 1983, archaeologists made almost 25,000 dives to the seabed to recover the shipwrecked *Mary Rose* and its contents.

East India ships

446 The *Batavia* was one of the first sailing ships to sink off Australia. Owned by a Dutch trading company, it ran aground on reefs between Australia and Indonesia. The dangerous seas in this area sank hundreds of similar ships, called East Indiamen, between 1600 and 1800.

447 At first, it took a year for an East Indiaman to sail from Europe to Indonesia. In 1613, Dutch captain Hendrick Brouwer pioneered a new route across the south Indian Ocean. This made use of reliable 'trade' winds, and reduced the journey time by half to around six months at sea. The *Batavia* was following this route when she was wrecked in 1629.

448 We know a lot about the *Batavia* wreck because the captain survived. He wrote a description of the ship hitting rocks – and what happened afterwards. With some officers, he set off in small a boat to seek help, leaving 268 passengers and crew sheltering on the islands. After they had left, a passenger and his friends attacked the other survivors.

◄ Strong gales and wild waves washed the *Batavia* onto hidden rocky reefs. With only wind to power their ship, its crew were powerless to avoid them.

▶ Archaeologists investigating the East Indiamen wrecks carefully record the positions of anchors, cannon – and boxes of treasure.

449 The *Batavia* mutineers killed 125 men, women and children. No one knows why. Perhaps they feared they would run out of food and water. When the captain returned with rescuers, after an adventurous voyage, the murderers were executed.

450 The wreck of the *Batavia* was discovered in 1963. It had sunk into a shallow reef and was overgrown by coral. This protected it and its contents from being scattered or swept away by waves and currents. Guns, anchors, ballast and parts of the hull all lay on the seabed in almost the same positions as when the ship was sailing.

▶ Sailors on board the *Batavia* used astrolabes to measure time and try to calculate how far they had travelled eastwards. Accurate clocks that worked at sea had not yet been invented.

451 Surprising things were found at the *Batavia* wreck site. These included a set of silver dishes for the Indian Emperor Jehangir and a carved stone doorway for the Dutch fort at Batavia (now Jakarta, Indonesia). Also found were four astrolabes (instruments used to plot a ship's position) and part of a globe showing the countries of the world known to Europeans around 1600.

I DON'T BELIEVE IT!

The 'trade' winds, used by ships like the *Batavia*, got their name because they always blow along the same path across the ocean.

Pirate wrecks

452 Spanish settlers in America sent gold and silver home to Spain, but many of their ships were robbed by pirates, wrecked on reefs or sunk by hurricanes. Only two pirate shipwrecks have been found. One is the *Whydah*, the other is the *Queen Anne's Revenge*.

453 The *Whydah* was launched in 1715 in London, England. It was named after the West African port, Ouidah (pronounced 'Whee-dah'). It was 31 metres in length, and needed a crew of 146 men. The *Whydah* was captured by the pirate Samuel Bellamy, known as 'Black Sam' because of his dark hair.

▶ Pirate captain 'Black Sam' Bellamy was only 29 years old when he drowned in the wreck of his ship *Whydah*.

BE A PIRATE

You will need:
square of bright red cloth

1. Fold the cloth in half.

2. Stretch the long side of the cloth across your forehead.

3. Tie the points of the cloth at the back of your head. Now you're ready to sail the stormy seas!

▶ Bellamy's loot, stored on the *Whydah*, included 180 sacks of gold and silver jewellery and bullion (pieces of gold and silver metal), and more than 100,000 gold coins.

454 Heading home to London in 1717 after its second slave-trade voyage, the *Whydah* met Bellamy. He chased it for three days then captured it. He then sailed the *Whydah* northwards, along America's east coast, robbing 53 ships he met along the way. The pirate crew on the *Whydah* came from many different lands including Britain, America, Africa and the Caribbean.

456 The *Queen Anne's Revenge* belonged to the pirate Edward Teach. He was known as 'Blackbeard' because he wore burning fuses under his hat to surround his face with smoke. In 1718, Blackbeard and his crew attacked the port of Charleston, South Carolina, USA, but were chased and fought by a British Navy ship. Blackbeard was killed, and the *Queen Anne's Revenge* sank near Charleston.

455 The *Whydah* sailed into a storm off Cape Cod in 1717. It was battered by 112-kilometre-an-hour winds and 9-metre-high waves. Bellamy tried to steer the ship away from the shore, but it hit a sandbank. It overturned, and smashed into pieces. All but eight of the crew drowned. When the survivors got to shore they were arrested and six were executed for their pirate crimes.

Ships' graveyard

457 **The seas around Cape Horn, the southern tip of South America, are the wildest in the world.** Fast currents, rocky shores, thick fogs, icebergs, roaring winds and massive waves up to 30 metres high make sailing difficult and very dangerous. There are 78 known wrecks charted at Cape Horn itself, with at least 800 more in the seas nearby.

ATLANTIC
OCEAN

CHILE

ARGENTINA

FALKLAND
ISLANDS

PACIFIC
OCEAN

Ships'
graveyard

Cape Horn

▲ The seas around Cape Horn and between Cape Horn and the Falkland Islands became known as the 'ships' graveyard' because so many great sailing ships were wrecked there.

458 **Why did sailors and ship-owners risk these dangerous waters?** To make money! In the early 19th century, before railways were built in the USA, the quickest way to reach California was to sail round Cape Horn. In 1848, gold was discovered there. The next year, 777 ships sailed round Cape Horn, carrying eager gold miners.

QUIZ

1. What disabled HMS *Edinburgh*?
2. What sank and wrecked USS *Arizona*?
3. What happened after the attack on Pearl Harbor?

Answers:
1. Torpedoes 2. Bombs 3. The USA joined Britain and its allies to fight in World War II

475 The attack on Pearl Harbor took place on 7 December 1941. American ships and planes were attacked by 353 Japanese aircraft, launched from six aircraft carriers patrolling the Pacific Ocean. The planes dropped high-explosive bombs, designed to smash through warships' armour plating. At the same time, five Japanese midget submarines fired torpedoes towards American ships from underneath the sea.

476 The raid on Pearl Harbor caused terrible loss of life. In total, 2388 Americans and their allies were killed and 1178 were injured. Today, the dead are honoured by a fine memorial, built out at sea above the wreck of the sunken US battleship Arizona. It lies undisturbed, as a peaceful grave for war victims.

▼ The wreck of the USS *Arizona* can be seen as a ghostly shape through the clear water of Pearl Harbor. The large white building is a memorial to all who were on board.

Shipwrecks today

477 Computers, electronics and scientific design make today's ships safer than ever before. Wrecks still happen though, often through human error. In 2002, the ferry *Joola* sunk off Senegal due to overcrowding. Over 1900 passengers died. In 2007, the *Pasha Bulker* (bulk carrier) was washed ashore in a storm in Australia despite shipping advice to seek safer waters.

I DON'T BELIEVE IT!

In 2004, a British warship was deliberately sunk to create Europe's first artificial reef. It will be a sea life refuge and a training ground for divers.

478 Mechanical failures still cause tragedies. In 1994, the ferry *Estonia* sank in the Baltic Sea, after locks failed on its bow visor (lifting door) and water flooded in. In total, 852 passengers died. In 2000, the Russian submarine *Kursk* sank with all its crew trapped on board because an experimental torpedo misfired. In spite of efforts to rescue them, all the *Kursk* crew died.

◀ Spills from shipwrecks can kill. Sea birds' feathers become matted with oil, so that they can no longer swim or fly. Fish and other sea creatures are poisoned, and beaches polluted.

499
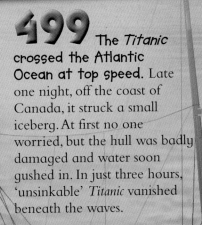

The *Titanic* crossed the Atlantic Ocean at top speed. Late one night, off the coast of Canada, it struck a small iceberg. At first no one worried, but the hull was badly damaged and water soon gushed in. In just three hours, 'unsinkable' *Titanic* vanished beneath the waves.

▶ The *Titanic* sank in very deep water. It was rediscovered in 1985 by French and American explorers. They found out that it had broken in two before sinking. Its hull had then been crushed by water pressure, scattering debris over the ocean floor.

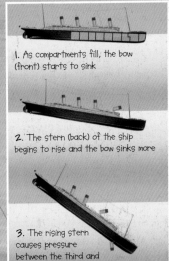

1. As compartments fill, the bow (front) starts to sink

2. The stern (back) of the ship begins to rise and the bow sinks more

3. The rising stern causes pressure between the third and fourth smoke stacks

4. The weak spot causes the stern of the ship to break off

5. The stern rests in the water before sinking. The sections came to rest on the seabed some distance apart

500
Shockingly, the *Titanic* did not carry enough lifeboats to save every passenger. Only 20 boats were on board. Some were launched half-empty, others were fatally overcrowded. The remaining passengers were either trapped on the *Titanic* and went down with it, or leapt into the water, where they drowned or died from cold.

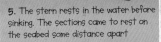

Index

Page numbers in **bold** refer to main entries; page numbers in *italics* refer to illustrations.

Index

Index